Child's Turn to Read

 Adult's Turn to Read

WE READ ABOUT

BASKETBALL

by KIM THOMPSON and MADISON PARKER

TABLE OF CONTENTS

SEAHORSE PUBLISHING

Parent and Caregiver Guide

Reading aloud with your child has many benefits. It expands vocabulary, sparks discussion, and promotes an emotional bond. Research shows that children who have books read aloud to them have improved language skills, leading to greater school success.

I Read! You Read! books offer a fun and easy way to read with your child. Follow these guidelines.

Before Reading

- Look at the front and back covers. Discuss personal experiences that relate to the topic.
- Read the *Words to Know* on page 3. Talk about what the words mean.
- If the book will be challenging or unfamiliar to your child, read it aloud by yourself the first time. Then, invite your child to participate in a second reading.

During Reading

 CHILD Have your child read the words beside this symbol. This text has been carefully matched to the reading and grade levels shown on the cover.

 ADULT You read the words beside this symbol.

- Stop often to discuss what you are reading and to make sure your child understands.
- If your child struggles with decoding a word, help them sound it out. If it is still a challenge, say the word for your child and have them repeat it after you.
- To find the meaning of a word, look for clues in the surrounding words and pictures.

After Reading

- Praise your child's efforts. Notice how they have grown as a reader.
- Ask and answer questions about the book.
- Discuss what your child learned and what they liked or didn't like about the book.

Most importantly, let your child know that reading is fun and worthwhile. Keep reading together as your child's skills and confidence grow.

WORDS TO KNOW

 basketball

 hoop

 pass

 shoot

 team

SIGHT WORDS

a	play	want
are	run	we
go	the	with
into	to	

We play **basketball**. CHILD

Basketball is played on a court that is inside or outside. ADULT

basketball

We run with the basketball. CHILD

As you run with the basketball, you dribble it, or bounce it over and over. ADULT

pass

We **pass** the basketball.
CHILD

You **pass** the basketball to your teammates.
ADULT

shoot

10

We **shoot** the basketball.

You can score two points if you **shoot** near the basket or three points if you are far away from the basket.

We want the basketball **CHILD**
to go into the **hoop**.

hoop

We are a basketball **team**!
CHILD

A basketball **team** has players who play different positions.
ADULT

team

Index

Written by: Kim Thompson and Madison Parker
Design by: Jen Bowers
Series Development: James Earley

Photos: cover ©2020 wavebreakmedia/Shutterstock; p.5 ©2019 Paolo Bona/Shutterstock; p.6 ©2015 glenda/Shutterstock, ©2019 A_Lesik/Shutterstock; p.7 ©2018 salajean/Shutterstock; p.8 ©2021 JoeSAPhotos/Shutterstock; p.9 ©2014 Monkey Business Images/Shutterstock, ©2020 Dmytro Zinkevych/Shutterstock; p.10 ©2020 Robert Kneschke/Shutterstock; p.11 ©2016 allensima/Shutterstock, ©2019 JoeSAPhotos/Shutterstock; p.13 ©2021 Marco Ciccolella/Shutterstock; p.15 ©2020 wavebreakmedia/Shutterstock

Library of Congress PCN Data
We Read About Basketball / Kim Thompson and Madison Parker
I Read! You Read!
ISBN 979-8-8873-5191-9 (hard cover)
ISBN 979-8-8873-5211-4 (paperback)
ISBN 979-8-8873-5231-2 (EPUB)
ISBN 979-8-8873-5251-0 (eBook)
Library of Congress Control Number: 2022945537

Printed in the United States of America.

Seahorse Publishing Company

www.seahorsepub.com

Published in the United States
Seahorse Publishing
PO Box 771325
Coral Springs, FL 33077